The Young Man's Guide

to Entrepreneurship:

16 Things You Need to Know

By: Chike Uzoka

DISCLAIMER:

This book is designed to provide advice on the subjects of Entrepreneurship and Business. The advice contained in this book may not be suitable for everyone. The author designed this information to reflect his personal opinion on the subject matter. The reader must carefully investigate all aspects of any business decision before committing themselves to it. The author collected the information contained herein from his own experiences and from sources he believes to be reliable, yet he neither implies nor intends any guarantee of accuracy. The author is not an authority in regards to providing legal or accounting advice; should the reader need such advice, they must seek out these services from a competent professional. The author particularly disclaims any liability, loss, or risk taken by individuals who directly or indirectly act on the information provided in this book. The author believes the advice contained herein is sound, but readers must take accountability for the actions they take or the resulting outcomes.

Additional information about the author and the book can be found at
www.chikeuzoka.com.

About the author

"In everything you do, have Passion & Purpose!"

Chike Uzoka is the Founder & CEO of Valentine Global, LLC, a consulting firm that specializes in Entrepreneurship & Business Coaching, Financial Counseling, and Mentoring for clients in New Jersey, New York, Pennsylvania, California, and Atlanta. He works with organizations such as The NAACP, Columbia University, The Children's Defense Fund, Black Enterprise, and Temple University. His interactive workshop series, "Handling Your Business," turns the classroom into an interactive boardroom where kids make real-life business decisions.

About this book

This guide is the book I wish I had before I became an Entrepreneur. I have a duty to share some of my experiences so that young men starting out don't have to make the same mistakes as I did.

"Each One, Reach One, Teach One"....

Glory to God for always being awesome and never changing.

To my mother, Ngozi Uzoka, for giving me what I've needed to get where I am, and to where I am going.

To my sister, Dr. Ifeoma Uzoka-Walker, for being my very first mentor and for looking up to me as her older brother.

To those who have ever supported an idea of mine and those who have seen the worst in me, yet still see the best in me.

To anyone who has ever chased an idea, a thought, or a passion.

Remember… "Passion & Purpose!"

How To Use This Guide...

This book is a guide created to give advice, direction, and action steps to young men thinking about owning their own business.

As you go through this guide, you can write down any notes, thoughts, and reminders to yourself (I've left space for you to do just that.)

I encourage you to write down anything that comes to mind, it could be worth a billion dollars! (Instagram?)

Contents...

Foreword...

About 2 years ago, summer 2010, I was just coming back into Newark, NJ from Miami, Florida on an early morning flight. My mind was racing and my pulse was beating a mile a second. I serve as the executive director of youth services and youth minister at Metropolitan Baptist Church. I am also the CEO of a non-profit organization; Dreams4Youth; and I had just completed fundraising efforts with the Alonzo Mourning Charity Foundation. When my pastor Dr. David Jefferson Sr. Esq. placed upon me a daunting task. He wanted to implement the vision for teaching and exposing young people to leadership through a camp environment for the summer months.

To say the least I felt a bit stretched thin. Leadership and youth had never gone together in one sentence as it relates to Newark, NJ youth. With the exception of Mayor Cory Booker and elected officials successfully changing the perception of Newark, the reality is statistics showed us that it would take time to change the academic environment and standard for our children. My co-director and I sat down and began to fill in the blanks of appropriate leaders in the community who were "called" to work with young people. I come from the school of thought that while several "work" with young people only a few are "called" to work with young people. Our dilemma was making sure we chose the right companies, consultants and people for the task at hand.

I recalled being at an event a few months earlier and meeting a young woman named Tiffany "The Budgetnista" Aliche. Tiffany was able to reach out to young people through her company and teach them how to handle their finances. At the time this was a major item of discussion for youth. Especially regarding youth being taken advantage of as the largest consumers. Tiffany shared that she would have someone working with her. She explained that his name was Chike Uzoka. As our Life Teen Leadership Day Camp kicked off, I'll never forget my first impression of Chike. His demeanor and smile immediately were contagious. His ability to share an idea and convey it to the young people of our camp not only impressed me but also showed me something greater. Chike was "called". Not in regards to the phone or any other communication device – his "calling" centered around making young people better. Helping them to improve their situation through sound doctrine and information. The result? More than 20 young people were exposed to his programming. Each of them improved in areas of understanding finances beyond measure. That summer the children met a mentor and I met a friend.

I'm not surprised one bit that he has written and shared a guide on entrepreneurship for young men. He's a giver and he shares. But if you're looking to get over, then this book isn't for you. Sadly you will be mistaken. This book is for the young person who is intent on creating a map, blue print or pathway to success. Chike shares the essential elements needed to lay down that foundation. He has created an interactive experience that put's you in the drivers seat. If you don't think and apply it doesn't work or serve its true purpose. It's up to the reader to implement their own plan.

I was extremely proud when I was asked to write the foreword to this book. Excited because I have seen the work Chike has been able to accomplish. From Teen Life Day Camp to our Freedom School for Boys all the way to his presence and leadership with our Youth and Young Adult Ministry his ability to work with youth is proven. I'm certain if you take the time to complete this book yours will be as well. I congratulate you for purchasing this book. It shows that you are serious about developing your essence. The essence of The Young Man's Guide to Entrepreneurship: 16 Things You Need to Know is now yours. It's yours to imagine and dream and create if you put your mind to it. So I encourage you to purchase a copy for your young person today if you haven't already. I'm going to make sure we implement it as a part of our Teen Leadership Camp. I will study it and work it with my children for generations to come. It's always a blessing to work with youth.

David Jefferson Jr.
Youth and Young Adult Minister
Metropolitan Baptist Church

1

Follow your instincts; it's where you find what you really want to do in life.

Chike-ism: Go with your gut.... all the time!

Message:

Your gut is that little voice inside your head that speaks from your heart. Do we always listen to it? No, of course not. It can't be that simple, right? Wrong! This is one of the hardest lessons I had to learn as a young entrepreneur, yet it has yielded the best returns! You should always follow your heart, just don't forget to take your brain along with it!

Action Steps:

Listening to your gut is not always easy, the more you do it the better you get at it, and it's the big difference in people who make decisions quickly, and people who don't.

Write down 3 things your gut tells you every day.

Notes:

2

Know before you Go!

Chike-ism: Do your research.

Message:

Doing research can be the difference between selling no products and selling 1 million products. It means you have to find information about your industry and its trends. Knowing the trends means knowing how to take advantage of them. This could sometimes be the most boring part of business; it's very crucial though!

Action Steps:

Researching your industry & its trends doesn't cost you anything except your time.

Use sites like Google, Bing, Yahoo, and YouTube to find information about anything!

Notes:

3

Convenience, Quality, or Cost… How are you better?

Chike-ism: Know what you're up against!

Message:

Competition will always be there. No matter how relatively insignificant a competitor may seem, their presence will always play a factor in the life of your business. Knowing your competition is the only way to realize your Competitive Advantage (what makes you different from the competition). I've made it a habit to deliver more service than I get paid for, which means more Quality for my clients. You can beat your competition in just one of three ways: convenience, quality, or cost. Choose one and choose wisely!

Action Steps:

Find out who does what you do, and then find all the ways in which you can do it differently and better.

List 5 competitors and what makes them good at what they do.

Notes:

4

Constant improvement is better than delayed perfection.

Chike-ism: Always be refining!

Message:

There is no such thing as perfection; but if there is, no entrepreneur has ever found it. You create something to the best of your ability, you get feedback on it, then you make it better – that's how it goes. Always remember the acronym KISS (Keep It Simple Stupid). Don't put too much into an initially "perfect" product or service, there will always be room for improvement. If I waited for this book to be 'perfect', it would never have come out.

Action Steps:

Nothing will ever be "wholly" perfect; instead, focus on perfecting each step as you take it.

Create a plan of action and put it into action! What are the next 3 things you need to do to?

Notes:

5

Teamwork makes the Dream work!

Chike-ism: No man is an island.

Message:

Having a team of mentors, advisors, and especially people who are where you want to be, is important for any business owner. No entrepreneur could have made it to their level of success without help from their partners, sponsors, investors, and other stakeholders. These folks help to keep you focused, put you in front of the right people, and remove roadblocks that might hinder your success. I am extremely grateful for the people that have helped me get to this point, their knowledge and advice has been priceless. Teamwork makes the dream work!

Action Steps:

People like Accountants, Lawyers, and Graphic Designers are key for your business to grow and be successful.

Start by asking people you know, who they know, then start putting together your team.

Notes:

6

If everyone is your customer, then no one is your customer.

Chike-ism: Know Your Customer!

Message:

Knowing your customer is something you must always be working on in business. In my Wall Street days, we were never allowed to make investment decisions for clients unless we knew them. Ask yourself: Who is my 'perfect customer'? Many businesses fail to answer this question BEFORE going into business. It's a huge reason why many businesses do not last more than 3 years.

Action Steps:

Research (yes, more research) and find about more about your potential customers.

Ask yourself: Who is spending money in this industry? How can I tap into that market? What product/service is missing? How can I fill the void?

Notes:

7

Become a marketing maniac!

Chike-ism: Know how to market!

Message:

People love to buy things, as long as they appeal to them. People will buy just about anything if it's marketed to them the right way. So long as they feel it fills a gap in their lives, they will pay for it. If something fills a need, the more likely it is that people will pay for it. I learned this important piece of advice when I took Economics at NJIT; it's what peeked my interest in business in the first place.

Action Steps:

Use your personal strengths to leverage your marketing strategies.

List 5 things you are great at doing.

Notes:

8

You are your Business!

Chike-ism: Your Personal Brand and Your Business Brand are connected.

Message:

People will buy from people they like, sometimes even if the product or service they're getting isn't the best. It's one of those human nature things. The man or woman behind a business is crucial to the success of any business. People generally love to know the personal side of a company; the personal side is one they can relate to. More often than not, this sense of familiarity will influence their buying decisions. I have seen this come up all the time in the business world; it's an important piece of knowledge to have!

Action Steps:

Be mindful of what you put out there and of your brand (personal and business).

Review your Social Media accounts like Facebook, Twitter, Instagram, Flikr, and Myspace and ask yourself: how would someone see me?

Notes:

9

It's nice to be important, but it's more important to be nice.

Chike-ism: Your ego will hurt you in business… and in life.

Message:

Your ego will get you nowhere, fast! If you plan on asking for money for your business, this is the one thing that will hurt you the most. As much as investors and banks love to give money to a great business idea, they also make their decisions based on your character... and no one really likes a bragger or a know-it-all. There's a fine line between confidence and being cocky – it took me almost 25 years to learn the difference!

Action Steps:

Practice being humble! Volunteering and giving your time for a cause is a great way to do that.

List some ways you enjoy giving back to people.

Notes:

10

A business that only makes money is a poor business.

Chike-ism: You have to know if your business can not only make money, but also enrich people's lives somehow.

Message:

Starting a business just because you love to do something isn't such a great idea. Turning a hobby into a business can be tough, and many times people don't ask themselves the vital question – will this business venture help change peoples lives AND generate revenue? If you can do the first thing really well, the second thing will come naturally.

Action Steps:

Determine how you're going to help people and make money at the same time.

Ask yourself: What product or service am I going to sell? How many people are willing to pay for my product or service? How can I reach the most people with my product or service?

Notes:

11

Your Network (and Knowledge) equals your Net Worth

Chike-ism: Who you know AND what you know!

Message:

Knowing the right people can prove priceless in business; however, what you know is just as important. What you know doesn't matter much if you don't know anyone who can use the knowledge. Seek out people who need the knowledge that you have. Everyone knows someone that you don't, and those are the people that you need to know. I am always networking, not to get new business cards, but to meet more people I may be able to help.

Action Steps:

The more people you can help with your product or service, the more they advocate for you and connect you to their networks, thus increasing your network (net worth).

List 3 people you are going to call this week and tell about your business.

Notes:

12

Having fun is good for business.

Chike-ism: Don't forget to have fun!

Message:

This is the fun one…. Have fun, that's it! Love what you do, or don't do it (as a business at least.) Having fun is essential in business, it allows you to be creative and puts energy into whatever it is that you're doing. People that have the most fun, make the most money. Real People Motors was started out of our sheer fun & love for cars – working on them, racing them, designing them, writing about them. Who doesn't love to have fun and make money at the same time?? (Answer: Nobody)

Action Steps:

Do what you love! By doing that, you'll do it well, and by doing it well, you'll make money doing it.

If you could make a million dollars doing anything, what would it be?

Notes:

Any questions?

You can track me down at

www.chikeuzoka.com

Yes, there's more!

The Greats and Not-So-Greats of Being Your Own Boss	
First, the Not-So-Greats…	*Now, the Greats…*
Salary: Not a secure paycheck	***Excitement:*** Adventure & Risk
Benefits: Pay for insurance yourself	***Originality:*** Create something that's never been created
Work schedule: Could be 24 hours a day	***Salary:*** Endless earning potential
Management: You make the decisions	***Freedom:*** Work wherever, whenever, however, with whomever
Risk: Venturing into the unknown	***Flexibility:*** Control your time

Notes:

Quick! Write down *at least 10* things you like to do; or make you happy: or things that make you feel more creative and empowered when you're doing them; or you just have fun doing.

Things I Enjoy Doing
Examples: Reading, playing an instrument, karate, sports, cooking, fixing things, cars…
1.)
2.)
3.)
4.)
5.)
6.)
7.)
8.)
9.)
10.)

(Reminder: Everything you write here is a potential business you own worth a million dollars!)

More questions to ask yourself:

What am I really good at?

What would I do for free?

What's missing in my life?

Am I ready to go against the grain/traditional/normal?

What do people know me for/as?

What can I make (legal) money doing?

What is my product or service? Can I explain it in 4 sentences or less?

What resources do I need to start my business?

Which resources do I already have?

Is my profit going to be seasonal or all year round?

Who am I selling to? Who is my 'perfect customer'?

Who is my competition and how am I different from them?

What risks are involved with starting this business? How can I minimize those risks?

What can I do in the next 3 days to get started on my business?

S.W.O.T. Analysis

Use the following 2 charts to list your personal and business Strengths, Weaknesses, Opportunities, and Threats.

Your strengths and weaknesses are internal, inside you; they are yours to control. Write down things you do well, things other people know you for, and things you can improve on.

Your opportunities and threats are external, outside of you; you have no control over these. Think about what trends you can take advantage of, what your competition is doing, and how you can turn weaknesses into opportunities.

Write down *at least 3* for each. Just write them down as they come to mind!

Notes:

S.W.O.T. Analysis (Personal)

Strengths...
What do you do well?
What do others see as your strengths?

Weaknesses...
What could you improve?
Where do you have less resources than others?

Opportunities...
What trends could you take advantage of?
How can you turn strengths into opportunities?

Threats...
What threats could harm you?
What is your competition doing?

S.W.O.T. Analysis (Business)

Strengths...
What do you do well?
What do others see as your strengths?

Weaknesses...
What could you improve?
Where do you have less resources than others?

Opportunities...
What trends could you take advantage of?
How can you turn strengths into opportunities?

Threats...
What threats could harm you?
What is your competition doing?

Some Lasting Advice from a Young Entrepreneur

1. Do what you love, and love what you do!

2. Surround yourself with people who motivate, inspire, and challenge you to be better.

3. Be yourself and trust your instincts!

4. Spend your time wisely; it's your most precious asset.

5. Don't wait to go after your Dreams!

6. You're an average of the 5 people you spend the most time with.

7. Take risks!

8. Share your knowledge with as many people as possible.

9. Entrepreneurs who have mentors have a much better success rate.

10. Never give up on your Dreams!

and…

11. Read # 1 again!

You can find me here…

Web: www.ChikeUzoka.com

Facebook: Chike EntrepreneurCoach Uzoka

Twitter: @chike_v

LinkedIn: Chike Uzoka

Amazon: Chike Uzoka

Made in the USA
San Bernardino, CA
08 December 2017